Animal Diaries
Life Cycles

A Dragonfly's Life

by
Ellen Lawrence

Consultants:

Susan Borkin, MS
Head of Life Sciences; Curator of Insects, Invertebrate
Zoology Department, Milwaukee Public Museum

Kimberly Brenneman, PhD
National Institute for Early Education Research, Rutgers University, New Brunswick, New Jersey

BEARPORT
PUBLISHING

New York, New York

Credits

Cover, © All Canada Photos/Alamy; 2, © alslutsky/Shutterstock; 4T, © arnoaltix/istockphoto; 4B, © alslutsky/Shutterstock; 5, © Steve Russell Smith Photos/Shutterstock; 6C, © SergeyIT/Shutterstock; 6–7, © John Sheil; 8–9, © Rene Krekels/FLPA; 9T, © Warren Photographic; 10–11, © Dwight Kuhn Photography; 13, © Dwight Kuhn Photography; 14T, © Dwight Kuhn Photography; 14–15, © Dwight Kuhn Photography; 17L, © Dwight Kuhn Photography; 17C, © Dwight Kuhn Photography; 17R, © Dwight Kuhn Photography; 18T, © Dwight Kuhn Photography; 19, © Dwight Kuhn Photography; 21, © rkhalil/istockphoto; 22T, © John Sheil; 22C, © Dwight Kuhn Photography; 22B, © Dwight Kuhn Photography; 23TL, © Steve Russell Smith Photos/Shutterstock; 23TC, © Dwight Kuhn Photography; 23TR, © Rene Krekels/FLPA; 23BL, © Steven Russell Smith Photos/Shutterstock; 23BC, © Corbis; 23BR, © Warren Photographic.

Publisher: Kenn Goin
Editorial Director: Adam Siegel
Creative Director: Spencer Brinker
Design: Alix Wood
Editor: Mark J. Sachner
Photo Researcher: Ruby Tuesday Books Ltd

Library of Congress Cataloging-in-Publication Data

Lawrence, Ellen, 1967–
  A dragonfly's life / by Ellen Lawrence.
     p. cm. — (Animal diaries: life cycles)
  Includes bibliographical references and index.
  ISBN 978-1-61772-594-4 (library binding) — ISBN 1-61772-594-3 (library binding)
  1. Dragonflies—Life cycles—Juvenile literature. I. Title.

  QL520.L39 2013
  595.7'33—dc23
                                2012019344

For more information, write to Bearport Publishing Company, Inc., 45 West 21st Street, Suite 3B, New York, New York 10010. Printed in the United States of America.

10 9 8 7 6 5 4 3 2 1

Contents

Watching Dragonflies

Today, I watched dragonflies at the lake near my grandpa's house.

Dragonflies are colorful flying **insects** with four wings.

It's spring, and the dragonflies are **mating**.

dragonfly

Joseph

head

wings

body

This dragonfly is life-size. Use a ruler to measure its length. How long is the dragonfly from its head to the end of its body? How long are its wings?

4

wings

There are about
5,500 different kinds of
dragonflies in the world.
Their bodies can be bright
colors such as emerald
green, ruby red, or
shiny blue.

eye

body

legs

Date: June 2

Dragonfly Eggs

Grandpa says that after mating, some kinds of female dragonflies lay their eggs in water.

Others lay their eggs on plants near lakes and ponds.

Today, I saw a female dragonfly laying her eggs at the lake.

She held onto the leaf of a water plant.

Then she dipped the tip of her body into the water and let the eggs come out.

lake

a female dragonfly laying eggs

A female dragonfly lays hundreds of eggs at a time. Then she flies away. She does not take care of the eggs or her young.

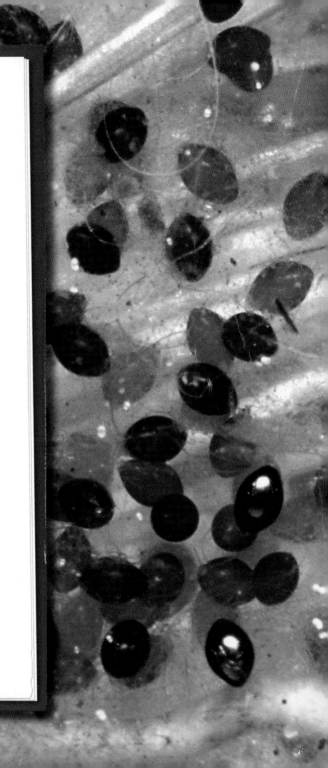

Date: **June 16**

Time to Hatch

Grandpa says that dragonfly eggs usually **hatch** in one to three weeks.

The baby dragonflies are called **nymphs**.

The nymphs must live in water because, unlike adult dragonflies, nymphs can only breathe underwater.

They breathe using body parts called **gills**.

Imagine you are telling a friend about dragonfly eggs. What words would you use to describe them?

a newly-hatched
nymph

a close-up photo
of dragonfly eggs

Some nymphs hatch
from eggs that are laid
on plants near ponds
or lakes. These nymphs
must quickly crawl into
the nearest water so
they can breathe.

Date: **June 30**

All About Nymphs

Today, we spotted a small, young dragonfly nymph in the lake.

It had six legs like an adult dragonfly, but no wings.

The nymph also had a hard covering called an **exoskeleton**.

As the insect grows, its exoskeleton gets too small.

So the nymph breaks out of it and there's a new, bigger one underneath.

Then the insect's body grows some more.

a young dragonfly nymph

When a nymph breaks out of its exoskeleton, it is said to be molting. A nymph may molt up to 17 times before it becomes an adult dragonfly.

exoskeleton

legs

eye

Look at this nymph. Think of some ways that it is the same and different from the adult dragonfly on page 5.

Date: **July 1**

A Growing Nymph

This afternoon, we saw a large, brown dragonfly nymph in the lake.

Grandpa said this nymph was probably one or two years old.

It had a long body and it had grown four small wing cases on its back.

Its wings are growing inside these cases.

Soon the nymph will leave the water to become an adult dragonfly.

A nymph's brown body makes it difficult to see among the greenish-brown water plants. This helps the young insect stay safe from bigger insects and fish that want to eat it.

A nymph's color helps it hide from its enemies. In what other way do you think a nymph's color might help it?

wing case

a two-year-old nymph

long body

legs

A Nymph Goes Hunting

Wow! This morning I saw the large, brown nymph catch a baby frog, called a tadpole.

The nymph's color makes it hard to see among the water plants.

The animals it hunts don't know it's there.

As the tadpole swam by, the nymph's long, grabbing mouthparts shot out and caught it.

The little tadpole didn't stand a chance!

nymph

tadpole

Dragonfly nymphs eat other young insects as well as shrimp, tadpoles, worms, water snails, and small fish.

grabbing mouthparts

nymph

eye

Date: **July 30**

An Amazing Day

Today, we saw the dragonfly nymph leave the water and climb up a plant.

Inside its exoskeleton, the nymph had changed into an adult dragonfly.

Its body had become much longer and it had grown four wings.

As the insect clung to the plant, its head burst from its brown exoskeleton.

Then it pulled its body out.

After an hour, the dragonfly used its new wings to fly away.

The nymph part of a dragonfly's life can last for just a few months or for about two years. Sometimes a dragonfly may live as a nymph for up to six years!

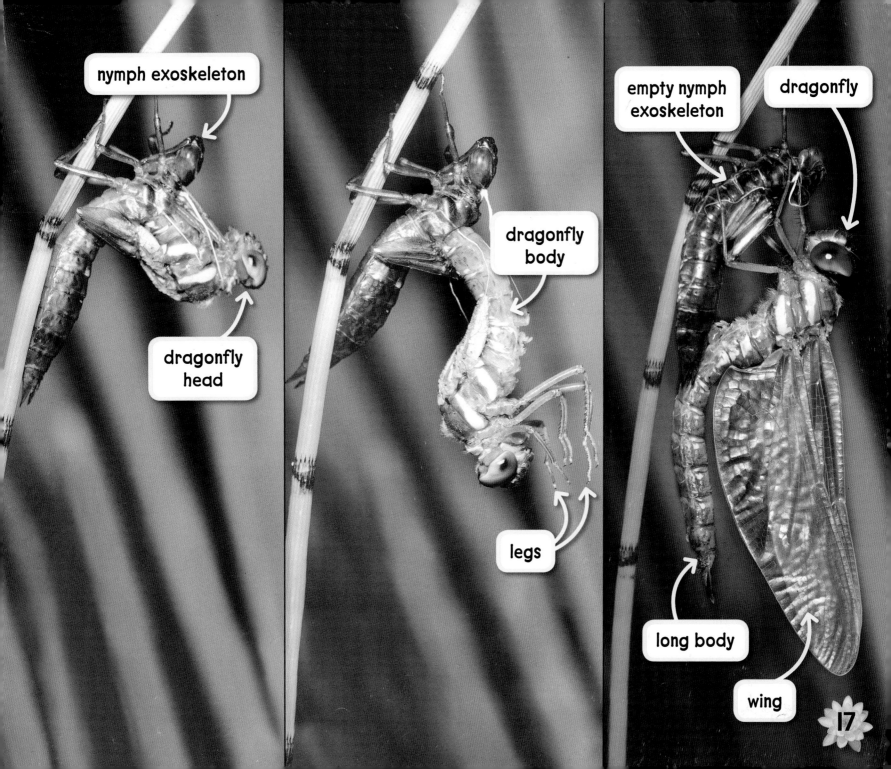

nymph exoskeleton

dragonfly head

dragonfly body

legs

empty nymph exoskeleton

dragonfly

long body

wing

17

Date: **August 14**

A Dragonfly Goes Hunting

A dragonfly was hunting close to the lake this morning.

Dragonflies eat insects such as flies, moths, mosquitoes, and flying ants.

Their huge eyes are able to quickly see the movement of another flying insect.

Their wings help them fly fast so that they can catch up to their victims.

Then they grab their meals with their legs.

eyes

Once a dragonfly has become an adult it breathes air through tiny holes in its body.

a dragonfly hunting

mosquito

19

Date: **September 30**

A Dragonfly's Life

It's been two months since I saw the nymph become a beautiful dragonfly.

Grandpa says that the adult part of a dragonfly's life is very short.

It may live for only about six to eight weeks.

In that time, though, the dragonfly will have mated, which is great news.

It means there will be more colorful dragonflies to watch at the lake in the future!

Dragonflies can fly more than 30 miles per hour (48 kph). They can fly forward and backward, and even hover in the air like helicopters. A dragonfly's flying skills help it avoid being eaten by birds.

Science Lab

Make a Dragonfly Diary

Imagine that you are a scientist studying the life of a dragonfly.

Write a diary about the dragonfly's life using the information in this book.

Include these life cycle stages in your diary.

- **A female dragonfly lays eggs.**
- **A nymph hatches from an egg.**
- **The nymph gets bigger and grows wing cases.**
- **The nymph changes into a dragonfly inside its exoskeleton.**

Draw pictures to include in your diary and then present your diary to friends and family.

Read the questions below and think about the answers.

You can include some of the information from your answers in the diary.

Look at the pictures. They will help you, too.

◀ *Where does a female dragonfly lay her eggs?*

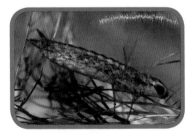

▲ *What does a nymph look like?*

◀ *What changes happen to the nymph when it becomes an adult dragonfly?*

Science Words

exoskeleton (*eks*-oh-SKEL-uh-tuhn) the hard covering that protects an insect's body

gills (GILZ) body parts that dragonfly nymphs and other underwater animals, such as fish, use for breathing

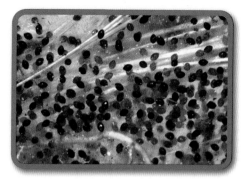

hatch (HACH) to break out of an egg

insects (IN-sekts) small animals that have six legs, two antennas, a hard covering called an exoskeleton, and three main body parts

mating (MAYT-ing) coming together in order to have young

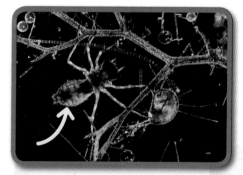

nymphs (NIMFS) the young of some insects, such as dragonflies and grasshoppers

Index

Read More

Allen, Judy, and Tudor Humphries. *Are You a Dragonfly? (Backyard Books)*. Boston: Kingfisher (2004).

Murray, Julie. *Dragonflies (Big Buddy Books: Insects)*. Edina, MN: ABDO (2011).

Smith, Molly. *Speedy Dragonflies (No Backbone! The World of Invertebrates)*. New York: Bearport (2008).

Learn More Online

To learn more about dragonflies, visit **www.bearportpublishing.com/AnimalDiaries**

About the Author

Ellen Lawrence lives in the United Kingdom. Her favorite books to write are those about animals. In fact, the first book Ellen bought for herself, when she was six years old, was the story of a gorilla named Patty Cake that was born in New York's Central Park Zoo.